experiencing DIVORCE

experiencing
DIVORCE

H. NORMAN
WRIGHT

B&H
PUBLISHING GROUP
NASHVILLE, TENNESSEE

978-1-4336-5025-3

Published by B&H Publishing Group
Nashville, Tennessee

Dewey Decimal Classification: 306.89
Subject Heading: DIVORCE \ GRIEF \ DIVORCED
PEOPLE

1 2 3 4 5 6 7 8 • 21 20 19 18 17

Contents

When Dreams Die

Hold fast to dreams
For if dreams die
Life is a broken-winged bird
That cannot fly.

Hold fast to dreams
For when dreams go
Life is a barren field
Frozen with snow.[1]

The haunting words of this Langston Hughes poem perhaps capture some of the emotion of divorce, as it did for a woman named Jean. She had been living her threefold dream as a wife, mother, and missionary. Along with her husband and two daughters, she was serving God in full-time, active service on a foreign mission field. Then one day she discovered her husband had been involved in an affair. With that knowledge, everything changed. Thus began a season of pain and struggle that eventually resulted not only in Jean's returning home from the life and ministry she loved and had worked toward, but returning home also as a divorced woman.

Her dream had died.

I had this vision that I was going to be married for the rest of my life. Now that vision was gone. For a long time, I had a mental picture that I was standing at a grave, trying to bury my marriage. The hole was dug, but boards were across the grave so they couldn't continue the burial because I refused to throw in my flowers. I was holding a dead wedding bouquet, my symbol of my marriage. I hung on to that bouquet for a long time.

I knew I was beginning to heal when the day came in my vision that I wanted to pick up some fresh pink carnations for myself and throw the dead bouquet into the casket. That's when I knew I was beginning to let go of my grief.[2]

Yes, dreams can be destroyed. Dreams can die. And few culprits are more adept at burying them than divorce. We do need to grieve over these dreams we've lost. The hurt is real, and the loss is devastating. But even dreams that have been thrashed on the hard rocks of divorce do not need to be left for dead. Dreams can live again.

Divorce has often been described—accurately, I believe—as being similar to a tornado. It can rip through your home with the potential for destroying not only every aspect of your own life, but also disrupting the lives of everyone connected with you. It stirs up a whirlwind of fear, anxiety, depression, and confusion. After the onslaught has done its worst, you're sitting there holding the pieces in your hands, even while time continues moving forward, leaving you broken and alone in its wake. Divorce is among the most wrenching experiences anyone can go through.

Whenever you experience a crisis of this magnitude, you are at first thrown off guard. You may temporarily lose your ability to cope. You seek a pain release, some kind of anti-memory pill, only to find that nothing of the kind actually exists.

But despite how it feels, divorce is not the end. You can regain your footing as you begin to understand what's really happened. You can learn to live again as you start to recognize the potential that lies ahead of you, even within this newly reordered set of circumstances. You can bundle this experience in such a way that it doesn't cripple or devastate you for the remainder of your life.

The primary purpose of this book is to provide guidance to those who have been through a divorce in the past or who have recently experienced one. In no way do I wish to minimize the sacredness of marriage or treat divorce as a typical, even therapeutic solution to one's unhappy life as a couple. As long as the possibility exists for a marriage to be saved and rescued, many blessings can still await those partners who each humble themselves, submit to godly counsel, and seek to offer their relationship as a testimony to what God can still do with broken things.

But if divorce has already happened, or if there's no stopping the will of one partner to see this marriage dissolved, I wish to convey an important truth that's often hard to locate from inside the cauldron of this tragedy. The prospect of continuing to live— even to thrive—remains for you to accept and embrace as an option. "'For I know the plans have for you,' declares the LORD, 'plans to prosper you and not to harm you, plans to give you hope and a future'" (Jer. 29:11 NIV).

In the aftermath of the storm, amid the ashes of a destroyed dream, God delivers hope that goes beyond your own resources and strength. It's not a shortcut. Not an easy path. But He does provide a way through. And in choosing to walk it, you can truly live again.

Chapter 1

Bracing for Impact

When does a divorce begin? Does it start when you visit an attorney for the first time? Not really. That's just the end result of something that began occurring long before, the emotional effects of which you've already been feeling.

This emotional experience of divorce is what comes from realizing you are no longer number one in your spouse's life; perhaps they're no longer number one in your life either. The process that brought the two of you to this breaking point may have taken years, but your acceptance of its reality, once divorce has become an unavoidable conclusion, is important.[3]

That's because the initial response to a marriage falling apart is often a sense of *unreality*. This must be happening to someone else, you think. Some have recalled feeling frozen in time. Numb.

Everything just stood still. Life suddenly stopped cold. Others have said it was more like a bad dream or a nightmare. They just wanted to wake up and discover it wasn't real. How could this happen? Divorce is something that happens to others . . . not to us . . . not to me.

But as unreality fades into harsh reality, the intensity of all the emotions finally hits. Their presence will come and go, but their arrival—sometimes predictable, sometimes quite unpredictable—can be painfully severe. For some, the devastation and intensity of emotions isn't much different from that of experiencing the death of a close friend or family member. As one man described it:

> Divorce is as close as you can get to death without actually dying. Only those who have experienced it can truly understand its dark power to test emotions and intellect to the ultimate degree. The only social trauma greater than divorce is the physical death of a loved one.[4]

This is what's often referred to as the *impact phase*. What happens when two cars hit each other? An impact occurs, resulting in damage. The same is true with divorce. As one person shared with me:

> It feels as though I was driving alongside a nice residential street in a new car, and all of a sudden someone backed out of a driveway and blindsided me. Not only that, they didn't stop to see what damage they did. They just hit me and drove off. So I'm left to deal with the damage all by myself. I feel victimized.

The "damage" you experience during this phase will depend on the length and intensity of the marriage, as well as on your feelings about having it end. If your ex initiated the divorce, you probably long for the relationship you once dreamed about, perhaps even had. This longing can become an obsession, dominating every waking moment. For others, however, the damage is mitigated somewhat by a sense of relief. Yet even in feeling this emotion, it may come with a corresponding constant of guilt, whether such guilt is specifically warranted or not.

Any of the following may happen during the initial week after you know divorce is impending.

- You may have difficulty concentrating. Your mind returns to the relationship, and you replay events and interactions again and again.
- You may stay by the phone or computer, waiting for a call, text, or e-mail.
- You may listen to sad songs, personalizing them to your situation—or you may hate hearing certain songs you once enjoyed, now that their lyrics sound so empty.
- You may spend time making plans for how you could try to reconcile, or you may focus on what's better now that you're removed from the situation, now that you're not continuing in the pain of this marriage.
- You may rehearse events and conversations to determine what went wrong, what you could have said or done, what you could have done differently, what the other could have done.
- You may recall the good times, wondering if any of the positive statements your ex-spouse ever made were true. *If they were true, how could this happen?*
- You may begin to doubt yourself, or you may concentrate only on the positive experiences and blank out the bad times.

- You may think of ways to get even, how to make your ex feel the same pain you do.

The impact of divorce on your equilibrium and emotions depends on many factors. But one thing's for sure: *you will feel it.* The love and care that once existed for you has dried up, vanished. Yet the other person still exists, and in many cases you'll still see them from time to time—perhaps frequently, if children are involved—creating ongoing reminders of the past that can make this whole situation even more difficult to handle.

But it *can be handled.* And part of how it's done is by accepting the reality that this kind of damage is normal. This fact alone won't make the impact hurt any less, but it will not be as capable of leaving you stuck on the side of the road, out of commission, totaled beyond all recognition of the person you truly are . . . the person you still can be.

CHAPTER 2

An Abundance of Losses

As you experience the loss of your marriage, you not only experience the absence of the other person. A number of secondary losses occur as well—things familiar, things you'd long taken for granted, things you tended to overlook in importance until they were suddenly gone and no longer a part of what was once your normal, everyday life.

But each of these lost elements of belonging must be identified, grieved over, and in some way let go. Think of the various ones you've experienced, like these:

- The couple relationship—all the activities you shared are gone
- All the rituals you did together—like daily text messages, phone calls, or weekend date nights

- The comfort and closeness you created, your physical relationship
- The feeling of having this person as part of your life, and of feeling yourself a part of his or her life
- Your hopes and dreams for the future
- Members of your partner's family with whom you bonded
- Gifts or affirmations you were accustomed to receiving
- The emotional, practical, and economical support you received on a regular basis
- Your former "couple" friends

What other losses have you already noticed and experienced? Be specific. In living without your spouse, are you now also living without your bill payer? Your gardener? Your chef? As well as your lover? One author who went through divorce described the dynamics of such losses in these general terms:

We may not think our spouses are going to war against us, but plans for divorce, and the completion of it, are often warlike. The spoils of this conflict are everything we treasure and worked hard for all our lives. The battlefield is in the most private and intimate recesses of our lives. It is a contest of wills and a battle of hearts and minds—all on our home turf. When love falls prey to hatred or apathy and the personal stakes are high, there are no dispassionate foot soldiers.[5]

When divorce occurs, you don't lose only this one relationship with your wife or husband. Many secondary losses actually come from losing relationship with others. That's because the alienation of divorce is more than just the withdrawing or separation of a person's affections from a former partner. When you enter into divorce, others will begin to draw away from you as well. Not all, but some. And even those relationships that stay intact can change, can become different.

So as if dealing with this loss isn't struggle enough, you probably won't have the level of support you want as you walk through the process. Your pain is likely to be intensified by the feeling that no one else really understands.

Perhaps you've come to terms with the fact that recovering from your divorce will take time, perhaps months. For some, it can take years. But many of those around you won't be so patient with you. They'll prod you with questions and statements, trying to get you back into the mainstream, saying things like, "Get on with your life," or "There are plenty of others out there who are better than what you had." Some of their comments and their lack of understanding will wound you. You may hear, "I told you so," or "You should have seen these problems coming." All of these comments can hurt. Few of them help. But many of them will occur.

Hopefully some of your closer friends will listen to you and help you through this journey of grief, but even the best of them may not be able to give good advice, simply because they don't know the answers. Some, even if well-meaning, can also give you bad advice.

So be careful what you ask your friends. It doesn't help to ask them why they think the divorce happened. How would they know? They don't have all the facts; they don't understand all the dynamics involved. Besides, your divorce most likely has come as a major shock to them. That's because while couples are together, they often do their best to present a rosy picture of how things are going.

Remember, a friend is a friend, not an expert. Their opinions tend to be colored by their own biases and life experiences. That's why, whenever others give you a suggestion or advice, you should ask yourself, *Does this advice seem guided by the Holy Spirit, or . . . ?* It puts a different perspective on what was said. (If you're feeling particularly bold, you might even ask *them* that question!)

Many have found that writing a general letter to friends is helpful, describing what is going on and what you're feeling. This gives you the chance to suggest to them the best way to respond, rather than just leaving you subject to unsolicited, undesired, inappropriate advice—which is not what you need. As you meet with friends or fellow employees who want to help, give them this letter instead of having to repeat your story again and again. They will be appreciative, since they often don't know how to act or what to say, and you'll likely receive a greater amount of healthy support as a result.

Yes, writing this letter not only helps your friends; it also helps you. Even if you never end up handing out a single copy, the exercise itself will enable you to verbalize what you expect and need from others.[6]

But recognize that realignments in these once established relationships are sure to occur. Some friends and family members will support you; others will not. These shifts of allegiances and alliances are among the many losses you can expect to follow your divorce.

But they are also among the things you can successfully navigate as you face divorce squarely, learn from it, grieve your losses, and prepare for better days ahead.

CHAPTER 3

The Divorce Process

Separating and divorce are not isolated, one-time events. They represent an ongoing process. Except for the death of a spouse, divorce requires more adjustments than any other stressful event in life. It involves completing mountains of paperwork, confronting a confusing legal system, handling all the symptoms of an ongoing crisis, fielding questions and suggestions from relatives and friends, and making an abundance of decisions in areas never before faced—often complicated by difficulties in finding the kind of trusted help and expertise you need.

One of the major issues that comes to light in this process is *identity*. "Who am I now?" When you've been married for some time, it's hard to think of yourself as anything other than a couple. How do you become a non-couple? Losing your couple identity will obviously take some work.

Prior insecurities you carried also intensify, even as new ones emerge, making you wonder where they came from. This is likely the first time in a long time your future has felt so open-ended—a reality that probably incites more fear and panic in your mind than intrigue and curiosity. All of these feelings leave you grasping for how to settle your identity.

For many, the time leading up to separation and divorce is the most volatile and painful period, bringing with it indifference, disillusionment, hopelessness, anger, discouragement . . . the list continues. There is convincing evidence, in fact, that the stresses of this period can result in a number of specific, negative repercussions. For example:

- Separated people have an increased susceptibility to viruses and other illnesses.
- Automobile accident rates *double* for people during the six months before and after separation.
- The divorced are more frequent users of mental health services, most commonly for problems such as anxiety, depression, anger, and feelings of rejection.

- The separated and divorced have higher rates of alcoholism, suicide, and involvement in homicides.[7]

So while many words of counsel could be shared in terms of how to manage this process, while maintaining a healthy sense of balance and identity, one of the best is a thought that may sound selfish at first, yet is necessary for survival. *You need to take care of yourself*—not only for your own benefit, but also (if you have them) for your children.

This is also a time of *transition*. Perhaps you can identify with the following description. I quote it at length:

During the transition phase, divorcing men and women usually become obsessed with thoughts about their former spouse and broken marriage. The history of the marriage is relived time and time again—the fights, the accusations, the significant events, the trivial occurrences that may have contributed to the breakup. When did the trouble start? Who is to blame? Was it inevitable? For some, the obsessive thoughts become maddening.

Although a minority of couples report they get along better once they no longer have daily contact, the majority report having primarily explosive and conflictual interactions after separation. The majority of divorced people studied have questions, at some time, whether they made the right decision to end the relationship. People vacillate between feelings of love and hate, longing and anger.

For many divorcing men and women, one of the most incomprehensible and frustrating feelings they experience is the continued pull toward an ex-spouse. Ex-partners think and wonder about one another and seek news about the other's activities. Some make excuses to call or stop by, some actively miss their former mates, some even pine for them. It is not only those who are left who experience this pull. Leavers experience it, too, and many find it incomprehensible.[8]

Following this season of transition, many then go through a period of *restructuring*—a time where they experiment with new activities, interests, and relationships. At first it may be frantic, moving too fast.

Still others allow their emotional wounds to remain open, giving in to fears by withdrawing from any future romantic relationship or by becoming very selective. Some, however, ease into this part of the process by daring to override their shaky insecurities, growing to trust and love again.

The last stage is *recovery*—and for many, it takes two years to get there. It's generally not something you can rush. But as one author described it:

> Those who successfully complete this stage have learned to accept the end of their marriage and the role they played in the breakup. They have disentangled their lives from those of their former spouses and created separate identities. They have achieved detachment from their former partners, so there is no longer a need for either hostility or dependence. And they have clarified their priorities, set realistic goals, and found a satisfying lifestyle.[9]

As a personal word of recommendation: One of the best steps you can take in walking through this process is by attending a DivorceCare seminar or support group. These are led by people who understand what you're going through and genuinely want to help. You will learn how to heal from the deep hurt of divorce and discover hope for your future, based on biblical principles. Go to www.divorcecare.org for more information and to find a group in your area.

Remember, this is a process, not something that can be quickly or easily patched up overnight. Expect it to take some time, but also expect to reach a point of clarity and contentment as you travel along.

CHAPTER 4

Initiators and Responders

Just as in marriage we each have different roles, we also end up responding to divorce in certain ways as well.

I use the words *Initiator* and *Responder** to describe these customary differences, although every couple possesses its own way of approaching things. None are purely textbook cases. Keep in mind also that an Initiator can have certain characteristics of a Responder, and vice versa. Not only that, the roles can sometimes switch back and forth, creating even more tension and immobilizing each person.

Most often, the Initiator is looking for the door, the way out. They're wanting to end the relationship. The Responder, however, is trying to block the other's way. They want to prevent this from happening. But even though for the Initiator the relationship is ended, they can also be plagued with guilt, realizing "I do want out, but . . ." There's an inner struggle.

Usually the problem of timing comes to the forefront. The Initiator claims to have been trying for months, even years, to get through to the other person—signs that they say the Responder has repeatedly ignored or simply hasn't picked up on. The Initiator says, "I need time and space. I love you, but . . ." The Responder, however, says, "Please don't leave me! What have I done wrong? Give me more time. Give me another chance. Why am I so unlovable to you?" The Responder has difficulty accepting the end of the relationship. The emotional pain of rejection is particularly intense and acute for this person.

Usually the Initiator wants to work on personal growth; the Responder wants to work on the relationship. But they never seem to get together. They're out of sync.

The Initiator has likely made numerous plans that the Responder knows nothing about, having left the marriage emotionally behind months before making any formal announcement. They may have been hesitant to leave since they know how much this will hurt their partner, but they know the marriage is already over. As a result of this internal conflict, however, their words or actions can seem oblivious, perhaps just a bit suspicious. Often their guilt intensifies, making them willing to give their partner *anything* if they can just call this marriage finished.

The Responder, on the other hand, spends more time on the emotional part, focusing on what's wrong with the marriage. But the more their spouse reiterates a desire to leave, the Responder ramps up their denial that anything is wrong. Soon, in most cases, the Responder experiences more anger than the other spouse. That's because they're probably feeling out of control, which is obviously highly frustrating to them. They're feeling rejection, and that hurts too. Their future has been turned upside down—taken away from them, in some respects, without warning. They're alone. Their financial life has been shattered. Fear is finding its hold on their life.

Another reason for frustration and anger is that the Initiator is in the position of advantage, having had more of an opportunity to develop a support network. The Initiator has usually planned his or her steps in advance. The person on the receiving end of the divorce, however—the Responder—is the one who's most caught off guard. They don't know what to do with these new feelings, where to go with what's boiling and bubbling inside them. They need a support network as well, but it's probably not in place, and the stress of exposing one's situation to others at such a point of desperation is overwhelming indeed.

In a few cases, couples could legitimately be labeled *Mutual,* possessing neither of the more clearly defined roles of Initiator and Responder. They've basically decided jointly to end the relationship. Other people might be surprised to hear this news; this is a couple who didn't seem unhappy from the outside. But on the inside, they both feel a separation or divorce is in the best interest of both. Together they are unhappy.[10]

A few questions to ask as you finish this chapter:

- In what way do you feel rejected?
- In what way do you feel guilty?
- In what way are you the Initiator?
- In what way are you the Responder?

*For greater detail and information on this subject, often referred to as Dumpers and Dumpees, see chapter 7 in *Rebuilding: When Your Relationship Ends* by Drs. Bruce Fisher and Robert Alberti. Also, *When the Vow Breaks* by Joseph Kniskern.

CHAPTER 5

Dealing with Thoughts and Memories

———✦———

Our lives are based on memories. Without them, we are somehow incomplete. Over time, however, memories tend to fade and become hazy, losing their sharpness. We may need photos or someone's reminder to activate them, while at other times they can be surprisingly recalled by simply a passing sight, sound, or smell. Memories are mysterious things.

That's why, despite our human memory's ability to function as sort of a storage container for actual events that happened in our lives, it also stores *emotional* experiences, which we often remember more easily than accurate facts.[11] And because much of the pain of divorce comes from memories—and because divorce is so heavily entrenched in emotions—our ability to move through the process toward healing must necessarily involve a strategy for dealing with this cascading variety of thoughts from our past.

Memories can serve at least two purposes: they can be *helpful* or they can *hinder*. When we learn from the past and make positive adjustments, that's how growth occurs. But traumatic and painful memories can bring the past into both our present and future in unhelpful ways.

The longer you were married, the more memories you possess, both good and bad—memories of what occurred and what didn't, of what was said and wasn't said. Some of these memories can stir up all kinds of blaming, explanations, apologies, confrontations. They can bring to mind defects you've long seen in yourself, as well as fodder for things you'd like to say to your ex-spouse. For many, the pain of these memories comes from what some call "thought addiction"—a condition that's reinforced the more you talk about the other person. Some even become addicted to talking about their addiction.[12]

But thoughts and memories cannot be allowed to control us in this way. We must deliberately strive, as Paul said, to take "every thought captive to obey Christ" (2 Cor. 10:5).

Certain things that are physically present in our homes, for instance, which once brought us great happiness, now produce pain. Some people have therefore found value in gathering up these mementoes and reminders, and putting them away where they can't be seen. Granted, you may struggle to think of getting rid of things that used to mean so much. You almost can't believe they're now able to generate such hurt. But don't discard them; just hide them. You can sort them out later, if you feel like it. In weeks or months your pain in relation to these items may be gone, or at least dissipated.

The same goes for certain *places* you used to attend. You may need to avoid them for a while. This can be especially difficult if you have children in school or sports, or if you're not really able to work around specific gathering places and appointments. But again, in weeks or months the pain these familiar venues generate may be gone—or at least manage-able—and you can more easily go back to doing what you once enjoyed.[13]

It's important that you *identify* these thoughts and feelings, not allow them to gain a foothold and to dominate your life. This is part of the process of healing and moving on. Here are some suggested guidelines to help you take an inventory of what may be residing within you.

- How you feel about losing the positive things in your marriage
- How you feel about losing the negative things in your marriage
- All the things you are angry and hurt about
- All the things you will miss about your ex and the relationship
- Everything you want to say "thank you" for
- Everything you want to say "I'm sorry" for
- Any significant statement about the relationship
- Everything you forgive your ex for.[14]

This last one—forgiveness—is something that most people have trouble with. You may not feel like doing it, but in time you will. *You must.* For you, too, said and did some things you shouldn't, and God's forgiveness has been vast and gracious enough to extend mercy toward you. Be careful not to fall into the trap of using memories to blame others for your current emotions. Remember, all of us are flawed, and all of us need forgiveness. Each of us can also *give* forgiveness.

Another way of taking control of your thoughts has been called the *bank book*. This is simply a notebook where you write down whatever comes to mind that you might want to say to your ex-spouse so you don't have to carry these thoughts around in your mind. This way, the next time you have a conversation with them, you can refer to the bank book rather than your memory.

This can include:

- A question you want to ask
- A solution you want to offer
- A promise you want to discuss
- An apology you want to make
- An angry statement you want to make

By writing these down, you may end up deciding it's a good idea (or *not* a good idea) to share what you've written. But writing them down gets them out of your head so you at least don't have to remember them. It helps you take control of your thoughts. It helps you eliminate rash comments and impulsive responses. It provides a cooling off period.[15]

For years I've encouraged those in grief to take a 3 x 5 card and, in as much detail as you want, write out what you're experiencing. You could describe the divorce that's happened, how it's impacting you, and how someone could be praying for you. Then whenever you run into someone or they call, you can either give them a card or read it to them. Having this written-out reminder will engage others in the best way to respond to you and will hopefully cut down on non-helpful responses. As said before, others will appreciate your guidance, and you'll be taking greater command over the memories and thoughts of your past, focusing instead on your present and future.

CHAPTER 6

The Pain of Divorce

To go through a divorce is to experience pain—perhaps the worst pain of your life. And the natural response to pain is to relieve it as soon as possible, preferably with a quick fix so we can get our life back in order. But in reaching out for whatever will work, we fail to adequately consider what the results of these remedies will be. Worse, we forfeit the opportunity to wait on God and to see what He is able to offer us.

The best way to respond is not by just avoiding or numbing the pain. When we deny the pain of hurt and try stuffing it into our subconscious, the mere fact that we're not thinking about it doesn't mean it's gone away. "Out of mind" does not mean "out of memory." Eventually the layers of hurt, confusion, and misunderstanding will make it more difficult for us to access the real reasons that caused the hurt to begin with. The pain simmering inside us, if not dealt with, will suddenly boil to the surface, resulting in the damaging emotion of rage. Or it will descend into the holding of grudges, keeping open an emotionally draining wound that we continually revisit, never letting it heal. Sound familiar?

The much better choice is to work on understanding why we are hurting and who can actually help us. We must think about pain in a different way.

Here's how one author put it:

> Pain guides us toward thoughts and ideas that we might otherwise push away, and it forces us to seek answers from places we've never looked before. Pain opens our minds to ideas that hold the key to new insight, understanding and freedom.[16]

Bottom line: pain has a purpose. It is actually God-given to protect us from hurting ourselves even worse, as well as to lead us toward depending more fully on Him.

Paul the apostle talked about dealing with a painful difficulty of his own—something he referred to as a "thorn in the flesh" (2 Cor. 12:7)—and how he begged God for the problem to be taken away. "But He said to me," Paul recorded, "My grace is sufficient for you, for power is perfected in weakness" (v. 9). Waiting on the Lord and trusting Him to be enough for us allows us to deal with pain in a redemptive, instructive, and healing way. In the end, we can come to Paul's same conclusion, that "when I am weak, then I am strong" (v. 10)—stronger in faith, stronger in Christ, stronger for the future.

The pain of divorce, I've already mentioned, is similar to the death of a loved one. Yet when death occurs, the physical loss of the person—though indescribably hard to bear and grow accustomed to—still moves us more naturally toward closure. Also, the support we receive from others at this time is usually rather effective, since people are more familiar with how to minister and care for others following a loss of this nature, one that they too have likely experienced in some way.

With divorce, however, your ex-spouse is still here. Moreover, if you have children, you're probably in for hundreds of encounters over the next few years. Your relationship is anything but closed; it's open-ended. And unlike death—a circumstance over which the departed person had little to no control—your ex made a choice to leave you. They wanted it this way.

So the pain of divorce becomes a visitor that overstays its already unwelcome welcome. When it first arrived, when you felt its first jab—especially if you were the Responder to this situation—the shock was immediate. You couldn't believe it. Outside were sun and billowing clouds, people going about their normal lives. But how could that be? How could things be so blissfully routine and ordinary out there when you're feeling so much darkness and despair in here?

Soon the initial pain was followed by a cluster of other painful feelings and experiences. These likely included (and perhaps continue to include) a sense of *emptiness, loneliness,* even *isolation.* The house feels emptier, not only around you but also inside you. Even when you're in the presence of others, invisible boundaries you've erected can cause you to feel walled off and alone. As author Doug Manning described it, "The awful loss of loneliness seems to be there every moment of every day. Loneliness comes in only one size—extra-large."[17] And along with loneliness comes the pain of simply not belonging, of feeling like a fifth wheel in nearly every circumstance.

Pain like this is emotionally draining. It makes you feel vulnerable, weak, and drained. You may sometimes feel hopeless and helpless. There are many days when you just want this experience to be history, to go away. That's normal. Trying to make sense of the nonsensical is understandable. But you must also want to make it profitable. You must be willing to *own* your pain, not deny or run from it, and allow God to transform it into something that proves healthy and transformative.

One step toward this goal is to begin taking clear responsibility for what you think and do throughout your daily life, including all your emotions and especially any negative feelings. You are better able to change and grow when you accept responsibility. The author of *Spiritual Divorce* writes:

> Taking ownership of our emotions is the only way to take back our power and regain control of our lives. We can't heal what we can't feel. Stepping into the storm of our turbulent emotions represents a sacred and significant time in our lives. It is during this time that we get to know our deepest selves. Standing in the storm of our emotions allows us to feel the

depths of our own woundedness and the agony of our broken hearts. It exposes our internal conflicts and challenges all that we believe about ourselves.[18]

The more natural response arising from separation or divorce, of course, is to focus on the wrongdoings and shortcomings of your spouse. Easier to point your finger at *them* than to focus on *yourself*, for fear you may sink into depression and regret—more pain.

Anger is a defense mechanism where you take whatever is bothering you and is wrong within you, and you project it on another person and blame him or her for it.

The problem with blame is what it leads to. Blame and anger work together to produce resentment. When you feed your anger with accusations and the self-justified shifting of responsibility, you will begin to burn with resentment. From resentment comes bitterness. Bitterness is a steady disease that eats you from the inside out, but selfdom affects the object of your bitterness.[19]

The only way to heal is by looking within, not by letting hurt and pain become anger and blame.

Another method of productively handling pain is what many have found useful—the writing of what's called a *tough love* letter to your spouse. This should not be an impulsive act, but rather one that is well thought out with prayer and with an honest, humble searching of Scripture. But if divorce is going to happen and nothing will save your marriage, this open sharing of what you're feeling and thinking is a useful way to handle the inevitabilities of pain. You're not just giving in to it; you're using it to cut a better road map into the future.

Writing this letter is a bold and responsible act—not of revenge but of tough, realistic love. The last thing you can afford to do if your spouse wants out of the marriage is to remain passive. They need to experience the disruption and consequences of their decision immediately. And this letter enables them to see the fruit of your pain in writing where they can read of it again and again. Many share this letter with their spouse in the presence of a third party, either asking that person to read it or even reading it to their spouse themselves in a calm voice.

Many concerns could be shared in this letter. You will have your own issues. The following extended excerpt from *When the Vow Breaks* is intended only to give you suggestions.

If true, share that you did not think of divorce as an option.

If true, share that you may have lost some of your perspectives because you were too close to everything, and because of that, you made mistakes, but not purposefully.

If your partner wants the marriage to be over, you will release them. You will no longer share your life with them unless there is a recommitment and both of you seek help.

If you don't want the divorce, it doesn't mean you're giving up on the marriage or your spouse by going along with it. You are honoring the decision your spouse has made.

When people ask about your marriage, you will be honest with them. You will be brief and will not assign guilt or blame, you will say the final decision is up to your spouse. If you disapprove of the divorce you will express that, but you will not resist this. If the divorce seems that it will occur, share that you hope there will be a peaceful solution. You would like to settle everything personally and not become overly involved with attorneys. They can be used to settle the court process.

Let your spouse know that continuing the relationship after the divorce will not happen except for necessities, and you will do everything possible to remove all reminders of them from your life. This is necessary because of their decision to leave the marriage. You feel that a separate life is the healthiest because of their desire to leave. Friendship would not work out. You will work on keeping your lives separate. Be sure to identify, clarify, and reaffirm your boundaries now and in the future.

Be open and honest about anything that you may have done to contribute to the crisis in your marriage, especially about your part and any regrets. If you need to ask forgiveness, do so.[20]

These are hard things to say; probably hard things for your spouse to hear. But they represent a suitable vehicle for expressing your pain, not simmering in it.

Most important of all, your bravery in trying to dig down beneath the nerve endings of pain, enough to see what's really causing it, allows God a solid opening for helping you receive His touch. Pain that's not *dealt with* will continue to deal you additionally damaging blows. Own it, and you can become strong enough, over time, to live with it . . . and beyond it.

CHAPTER 7

The Grief Process

With any loss, grief tries to take over, attempting to hold us perpetually hostage while it flits in and out of our lives. We experience it psychologically through our feelings, thoughts, and attitudes, as well as socially through our ongoing interactions with others. The grieving experience is also physical. Sadness results in bodily symptoms that impact our health. Our body grieves; our mind grieves.

Grief is also a very personal experience. We alone must ultimately endure it, and we require no one else's permission to go through it. The loss that precipitates it does not need to be accepted or validated by others for us to know, experience, and express grief.[21]

So as hard as the process can be, grieving is still normal—a natural, predictable, expected reaction to loss. The *absence* of grief, in fact, is what's abnormal.

- Through grief we express our feelings of loss. And there are many losses.
- Through grief we express our protest at the loss, as well as our desire to change what happened and have it not be true. Many get angry at their grief.
- Through grief we express the effects we have experienced from the devastating impact of the loss.[22]

But it's fair to ask why. Why must we go through this experience of grief? What is its purpose?

The purpose of grieving is to get beyond these reactions so we can face the loss and then work toward adapting to the changes so we can live with the loss in a healthy way. We start with, "Why did this happen to me?" Eventually we move on to, "How can I learn through this experience? How can I go on with my life?" When the "how" questions replace the "why" questions, we know we've started to adapt to the reality of the loss. "Why" questions reflect a search for meaning and purpose in loss;

"How" questions reflect a searching for ways to adjust to the loss.[23]

Perhaps you've been in the grief process for a while now, following your divorce. If so, you'll need to address two questions at some point:

1. *Have you committed yourself to a certain amount of time to grieve?* Some do so intentionally, some unintentionally. But don't let any suggested time frames dictate your own period of recovery. Don't set a time frame unless it's all the time you need. Keep it open-ended.

2. *Have you given yourself permission to stop grieving at a given point in the future?* People in grief do need to give themselves permission to grieve, but also permission to *stop* grieving. Throughout grief, you are saying good-bye to the one or to what you lost. Eventually, however, the passage through grief takes you to where you can say hello to something new or different.

How *do* you say good-bye when a part of you doesn't want to say good-bye? Even the person initiating the divorce can have a mixture of feelings. Part of you wanted to leave; part of you didn't.

Perhaps the following exercise will prove helpful, even though it can take some time and thought to complete. Give yourself a week to begin a list of the many *positives* that, because of divorce, you'll need to resign now to the past. Add to it day after day as new ones come to mind. Then take a second week to create a list of *negatives* related to your marriage and spouse that need to be told good-bye. Once you've finished, set aside an extended time of prayer where you can lift these lists before the Lord, symbolically releasing them from your life into His care and keeping. Say good-bye to what cannot come back; forgive and release what now needs to be forgotten and moved on from.

Here's another exercise as well. One of the most common barriers to completing the grief process after any loss is the "If only" statement—"If only I had . . ." "If only I hadn't . . ." "If only it could have been different." Some will tell you to get rid of your "if only" statements, but I believe dreaming about the way things could have been is helpful in being able to more fully identify all you've lost. No one else can do this *for* you, but you can do it yourself in a number of ways. For instance, you can write a story about the way you think your marriage should have gone, or you can complete a series of "I wish" statements like these:

- I wish I (or they) had . . .
- I wish I (or they) hadn't . . .
- I wish I (or they) had said . . .
- I wish I (or they) hadn't said . . .
- I wish they would say to me today . . .
- I wish they wouldn't say to me today . . .

But for grief to be complete, for your good-byes to bring closure, one other step is imperative—and it's admittedly a hard one. I've mentioned it on more than one occasion already. *Forgiveness.*

Some of the unfinished business that grief accentuates are the hurts and offenses caused by the one we've lost (in this case, by the one who divorced you). Memories, as discussed previously, allow us to carry vivid recollections of past events, and the most hurtful memories can grow to be a tremendous burden, continuing to inflict torment on us. But their power is fueled by our refusal to let go. Hanging on to them and revisiting them will poison our present and ravage our future. *The solution is forgiveness*—because when we release the person, we too are released. If we don't forgive, we sentence ourselves to the prison of resentment.[24] (See Jesus' parable on this subject in Matthew 18:21–35.)

In order to move forward, you simply must resolve and release your resentments. Write them out, if necessary. List them all—in as much detail as possible. And when you feel you've reached an end, consider what one author suggests: "Imagine your spouse sitting in a vacant chair and you say everything that you would like to say to them. You can even switch chairs and say things they would say back to you. Then go back to your chair and say the things that you would like to say again."[25]

You might even want to write these resentments in a letter that you never intend to mail. (Sometimes written sharing is more helpful than verbal.) But the purpose is not to keep blaming your ex-spouse; it's to put your finger squarely on what you are purposing in your heart to forgive.

You may be thinking, *What if I choose not to forgive?*

"If you don't forgive" says Doug Easterday, "what you're saying by the inference of your action is what that person did to you is more important to you than going on with God. There isn't anything that someone could do to you that would be more important than going on with your personal relationship with Jesus Christ."

If you don't forgive, you create a barrier between God and you. Holding unforgiveness in your heart is a sin. Dr. Myles Munroe says, "If you don't forgive, you cannot even pray. So if you are divorced and you still harbor bitterness in your heart toward that person who was in your relationship previously, then you have literally cut off your relationship with God. You have hindered your prayer life, and there is therefore no way you can actually ask God to heal that person or change that person because He can't even get through to you. Forgiveness is the key to getting on your way to healing because God can heal you only if He can reach you, and He can only get to you if you have forgiven the person who hurts you."

You are blocking yourself from the power of answered prayer when you choose not to forgive. "If I had cherished sin in my heart, the Lord would not have listened" (Ps. 66:18 NIV).[26]

Grief must have its day. The process cannot be worked around or avoided. But it can be lived through and be allowed to reach closure if you give it time to work, if you give it permission to end, if you identify what needs to be told good-bye, and if you forgive what will only keep holding you back. And God can help you do *all* of these. "My mind and my body may grow weak," the psalmist said, "but God is my strength; he is all I ever need" (Ps. 73:26 GNT).

CHAPTER 8

Finding Stability

Stability. After all the tremors brought on by divorce, you crave the almost forgotten experience of feeling stable, settled, not constantly being scattered and out of sorts.

But what can give you stability? Relying upon the Lord and the Word of God is definitely a priority. Stabilizing your spiritual life is a foundation. What occurs spiritually can counter the emotional energy that is being drained from you at this time.

For even with all the areas of pain and loss you've borne and could identify firsthand, you may not be completely aware of just how deep the trauma has actually gone. You've been left with a broken heart, for instance. The bonds of a significant relationship have been torn apart, with no quick way to repair the breakage.

But there is hope in Christ. Steve Grissom and Kathy Leonard, in their book *DivorceCare,* write: "A healing relationship with Jesus is available today for everyone who believes, regardless of what that person has done in the past. He alone can heal your broken heart."[27] As Jesus said in some of the first words of His earthly ministry, reading from a portion of Isaiah's prophecy, "The Spirit of the Lord is on Me, because He has anointed Me to preach good news to the poor. He has sent Me to proclaim freedom to the captives and recovery of sight to the blind, to set free the oppressed" (Luke 4:18).

In addition to a broken heart, you've also endured a broken spirit and a bruised, painful soul. Divorce has overshadowed everything else that's occurred in your life, and the instability has gone far beneath the surface. Here's how one person described it:

> I felt like all of my blood had turned to ice. My heart was racing. I thought that I was going to get sick. I remember having this feeling that a big hole had opened up underneath me and that I was sinking down into it, and I couldn't find my way back up. I felt like my heart and my soul had been pulled out.[28]

Perhaps you know the feeling. But the Word of God can be a source of healing and revival for you. In the familiar words of Psalm 23, we read that "he makes me lie down in green pastures, he leads me beside quiet waters, he refreshes my soul" (vv. 2–3 NIV). For "the instruction of the LORD is perfect, renewing one's life; . . . the precepts of the LORD are right, making the heart glad; the command of the LORD is radiant, making the eyes light up" (Ps. 19:7–8). Much of your stability can be retained and maintained by spending time daily in the Bible, being fed, nourished, and replenished by the Lord and by His truth.

Even giving yourself permission to cry is a way of stabilizing your turmoil of heart and mind. The solvent of tears can bring balance to your emotions. The tears you shed may be few on occasion, or they could perhaps be a torrent. But they truly have their own language. Tears even release chemicals that relax the nervous system. Crying is a healthy expression of hurt that releases a multitude of emotions, enabling you to settle out on the other side.

Another source of stability comes from friendships. "Two are better than one because they have a good reward for their efforts. For if either falls, his companion can lift him up; but pity the one who falls without another to lift him up" (Eccl. 4:9–10). Building, renewing, and deepening same-sex friendships will help fend off loneliness, providing you a good outlet for staying grounded and accountable.

And as far as building new opposite-sex relationships? The best advice is to *wait*—wait until you've healed enough to accept being single in a positive way. How long will this take? Difficult to say. We all differ in the grief and recovery process. But when in doubt about starting to pursue something more serious with someone of the opposite sex, lean first on the wise counsel of *waiting*. You'll be better prepared by staying patient. You probably need time to foster your stability more than you need somebody else right now. Again, use regular moments of study and Scripture reading to rebuild the base of truth and confidence beneath you.

I like how Grissom and Leonard say it:

When human life is threatened by serious injury, a medical system is activated to provide help. Patients are sped to an emergency room to stabilize their condition and to get a diagnosis of what is wrong. Recovery might take months or years, but a health care system is in place to help the patients each step of the way.

The emotional damage from divorce can be just as traumatic, just as devastating as physical injury, but the help system for divorce traumas is not as apparent. There is no hospital emergency room to go to. Yet if you read God's word in the Bible, you will find that a different kind of help system, or emergency room, exists, and it's up to you to discover more about the healing offered there. Just as God restored and healed the nation of Israel in the Bible, He promises to heal your wounds as well. Can you trust the promises of God?[29]

Absolutely yes!

CHAPTER 9

Anger

It's true that you can hold back and bottle up your emotions . . . for a while. But not for long. If you don't let them out, you'll discover they will find their own means of expression. Your storage capacity for them is only so large. It has limits. And when it's full, feelings spill out, causing confusion, turmoil, or even a rash of physical ailments. Your emotions can end up controlling your life.

Primary among these emotions is usually *anger*. Anger has the potential and power to override all your other feelings. Anger can destroy your relationships, your future, and yourself. Even by trying to hold it in, everyone can be hurt—you and everyone else.

Anger is a strange, puzzling emotion. Obviously, it's a strong feeling of irritation. We've all felt and received that. But it's also a signal and warning system telling you that something more is going on in your life than you're paying attention to. If you ignore this signal, you do so at your own peril, because anger is not like a postcard sent at a bulk rate. It's more like a special delivery letter telling you in direct, personal language that you are being hurt, your rights are being trampled, you're living in fear, you're frustrated, or you're ignoring something significant in your life. So what can you do about it?

The better question to ask first is not *what*, but *why*—why are you experiencing so much anger at this time?

Truly, few categories of anger are higher on the scale than divorce anger. If you're like most people, the dynamics that led up to this situation mean you've been collecting hurt and frustration and unfulfilled expectations for a long time—losses and disappointments and broken promises, feelings of being exploited and betrayed. You could probably add more. The authors of *Rebuilding When Your Relationship Ends* describe it this way:

> Divorce anger is extreme. Rage, vindictiveness and overpowering bitterness are common

feelings when a love relationship is ending. It is a special kind of anger that most of us have never experienced before. Married friends don't understand the strength of it unless they too have ended a love relationship.[30]

Few of us, therefore, require any real convincing that the anger sparked by divorce is unlike any other. Another writer takes the thought even further:

Anger and divorce go together about the same as do love and marriage. As long as you hold on to your anger, you will be bound to your ex as surely as if you were still in love; the only difference is that the bonds will be negative rather than positive. For your own sake, you need to eliminate both the positive and negative bonds with your former partner.[31]

Each of these observations leads us back to a desire for dealing redemptively and creatively with our anger. Ignoring it or telling it to go away won't work, of course. Even judging it and telling yourself it's wrong isn't much help. Only by turning its energy into a gift does anger become something constructive in our hands toward building a better life.

Basically, there are three ways of dealing with anger: repress it, suppress it, or express it.

To *repress* anger means to never admit you're angry, to simply ignore its presence. This repression is often unconscious, but it is definitely not healthy! Repressing anger is a vain attempt at burying it alive . . . and someday there will be a resurrection.

To *suppress* anger is more common. This is when you're aware of being angry, but you choose to hold it in and not let others know. Responders tend to hold in their anger for fear it will keep the other person away. Initiators tend to hold it in because they feel guilty.

Suppressing anger, let's be clear, does have some merit. The Bible says, "Good sense makes a man restrain his anger, and it is his glory to overlook a transgression or an offense" (Prov. 19:11 AMPC). Nehemiah once wrote about a situation in which he became "extremely angry" when he heard about some people's "outcry and these complaints" (Neh. 5:6). But "after seriously considering the matter"—another version says "I consulted with myself" (v. 7)—he rerouted his anger into a form that produced positive results. Whenever suppressing anger provides you space to relax, cool down, and act in a more rational matter, that's a wise thing. Eventually, though, the anger needs to be recognized and drained away in a healthy manner. The person who always stuffs their anger becomes a sad case, indeed.*

The goal is to achieve an ability to *express* your anger. Putting your feelings and thoughts into words gives them shape and meaning. It also gives you the freedom to overcome them.

The best way to give vent to your anger is by telling it to God. Contrary to popular spiritual opinion, God wants you to express your anger. "Be angry and do not sin," the Bible says. "Don't let the sun go down on your anger" (Eph. 4:26). Out-of-control anger that leads to raging, throwing things, verbal abuse, or acting out in other inappropriate ways is obviously wrong. When anger becomes aggressive, it leads to sin, to yelling, to harsh words, to swearing, all with tremendous emotion. But by releasing this anger and frustration in prayer to God, you overcome the temptation of either soaking in bitterness or exploding in violent tantrums.

Many have found writing in a prayer journal to be a beneficial exercise. As you write, you discover more about your anger and yourself than you ever thought possible. You may even find throughout this process that your anger is covering and masking other emotions. Anger has a way of feeling safer than fear, hurt, and guilt. That's why we often go there as a way of not having to tackle more foundational issues that are harder to work with. An additional benefit of journaling—both for yourself and for others—is that the things you write in your journal become things you probably won't take out on your family and friends. Praying through it with pen and Bible in hand is a positive approach to letting God help you with your anger.

But being able to express your anger in healthy ways to others is necessary as well, not carrying all the weight around by yourself. An important distinction to remember here is to focus your anger on actions, not on people. Instead of saying, "You make me so angry," you can tell him or her, "You acted in this way, and I *felt* angry because of the way you behaved."[32]

Another reason for expressing your feelings is because it sends a clear message to everyone around you that tells them exactly how you're doing. If you're silent and stoic all the time, they'll think you're getting over it and doing just fine, which is often not an honest assessment.

Sometimes anger can sway back and forth from anger toward yourself to anger toward your ex. At other times, you may be tempted to respond with silent anger. Passive-aggressive anger—such as giving the silent treatment, purposefully forgetting, not following through on a task, ignoring requests, procrastinating—is always counterproductive. Anger expressed in a vindictive way is never helpful. But crying, even yelling (in a private room), writing non-mailed letters, using the empty chair technique, investing in physical exercise—each of these can be helpful in getting anger out of your system in profitable ways.

Hurt is emotionally draining, so we often turn to anger in hopes of protecting ourselves. But we usually only succeed at building walls that keep people out, while keeping all our anger inside. It doesn't bring any healing, only more alienation. Of all the ways you can handle your anger, only by choosing ways to express it to God and others does it ever come out of its protective shell where it can be turned into a stepping-stone toward positive outcomes.

---

*Perhaps my book *A Better Way to Think* would provide you helpful insight on talking to yourself in ways that are more productive, not damaging.

CHAPTER 10

Depression

I try to do what I need to be doing, but I'm immobilized. The days are gloomy, no matter how bright. The nights seem endless. Apathy blankets me like a shroud. I eat because I have to, but there is no appetite or taste. I feel as though a massive weight is on my shoulders, and fatigue is my constant companion."

This is the painful cry of a person in the throes of a gripping depression.

Divorce brings with it many companions, most of which you don't want. One of these is *depression*. If you already tended toward depression even before experiencing a crisis like divorce, you can expect your depression to be intensified now. The feeling of despair in such a major loss is understandable. You can deny it, bury it, feed it, ignore it, but it will probably continue to float in and out of your life in some form. The cry of the psalmist to God may reflect your feelings just now: "Don't turn away from me, or I will die" (Ps. 143:7 NLT).

Depression makes each day seem as though the dark clouds are here to stay. Apathy blankets you like a shroud; withdrawal becomes a lifestyle. When depression hits, your perspective leaves. It alters your relationships because you're oversensitive to what others say and do. The future looks dismal. A sense of hopelessness has invaded your life. And the deeper the depression, the more paralyzing your sense of despair. You feel passive and resigned. Everything seems out of focus.

Losses are at the heart of depression. Depression and losses are inseparably connected. And the greater the loss, the deeper the depression can become.

Any loss can trigger a reactive depression, whether a concrete loss like a job, a home, a car, a valued photograph, or a pet. Especially devastating, however, are those losses that take place in your mind—the loss of love, hope, ambition, self-respect, the death of a dream, or other intangible elements of life. Losing any kind of love relationship is hard, particularly on women, who more naturally put so much of themselves into their relationships and build such strong attachments. Here's how Maggie Scarf describes this dilemma in her classic book *Unfinished Business*.

> It is around *losses of love* that clouds of despair tend to cover, hover and darken. Important figures leaving or dying; the inability to establish another meaningful bond with a peer-partner; being forced, by a natural transition in life, to relinquish an important love tie; a marriage that is ruptured, threatening to rupture, or simply growing progressively distant.[33]

Truly, what loss is any greater than divorce? For the stronger the attachment, the more intense the feelings of loss.

The symptoms of depression vary from person to person. Perhaps depression is new for you, or it may have been a constant companion for years. Either way, it will typically come with feelings of sadness, hopelessness, guilt, a sense of indifference ("who cares?"), of worthlessness, as well as changes in sleeping and eating patterns. Another characteristic of depression I've often heard expressed is by those who say, "I feel alone, and I don't know if anyone understands."

At least verbalizing these feelings is better than stifling them down. David and the other writers of the psalms verbalized depression numerous times in their various songs and poems, as in the chapter that says,

> I am like a man without strength, abandoned among the dead. I am like the slain lying in the grave, whom You no longer remember, and who are cut off from Your care. . . . Your wrath sweeps over me; Your terrors destroy me. They surround me like water all day long; they close in on me from every side. You have distanced loved one and neighbor from me; darkness is my only friend. (Ps. 88:4–5, 16–18)

David, looking back on a time of deliverance in his life, still recalled the depths he'd once felt: "I waited patiently for the LORD, and He turned to me and heard my cry for help. He brought me up from a desolate pit, out of the muddy clay, and set my feet on a rock, making my steps secure" (Ps. 40:1–2).

If sleep has become a problem because of your depression, consider reading Scripture out loud before you turn out the light. God's Word will make

a difference, and your spiritual life will be affected.
Here are some selected passages that may be helpful:

> When you lie down, you will not be afraid;
> you will lie down, and your sleep will be pleas-
> ant. Don't fear sudden danger or the ruin of
> the wicked when it comes, for the LORD will
> be your confidence and will keep your foot
> from a snare. (Prov. 3:24–26)

> I lie down and sleep; I wake again because the
> LORD sustains me. (Ps. 3:5)

> If I'm sleepless at midnight, I spend the hours
> in grateful reflection. (Ps. 63:6 MSG)

> When I am filled with cares, Your comfort
> brings me joy. (Ps. 94:19)

> I will both lie down and sleep in peace, for
> You alone, LORD, make me live in safety. (Ps.
> 4:8)

Like grief, depression is a journey, though it feels
more like a long, exhausting trek through an arid
desert. But while you may feel as though you're

walking completely alone, many others have actually passed this way before you. Cling to the following words as both an acceptance of what you're currently feeling, as well as a vision of well-placed hope in God for your future.

> Why are you in despair, O my soul? And why have you become disturbed within me? Hope in God, for I shall again praise Him for the *help of His presence*." (Ps. 42:5 NASB, author's italics)

CHAPTER 11

Fear and Worry

Your daily habits will need to be adjusted now that your spouse is gone and moving out. You were accustomed, of course, to spending *limited* time apart, even when your spouse was still in the relationship. But now you're all alone, whether you want to be or not. So loneliness can set in, as well as the misapplied belief that says, "I'm going to be like this forever." This is just one of the many fears that may threaten to dominate your life.

Truly, when divorce is impending or has already occurred, you can expect to be plagued by an invasion of fear.

What are some of the fears that have crept into your life? Perhaps they were already present beforehand to some degree, but the shock and separation of divorce have heightened them to a whole new level.

Many say, "I'm afraid of the future. I don't have any certainty. It's all unknown." They have difficulty seeing themselves functioning as a single or unmarried person. "How can I adjust to being alone?" You may feel emotionally stuck, fearing you can no longer participate successfully in many of life's activities and experiences.

Another natural concern is the fear of a label— "I'm a divorced person now. What does than say about me? What will others think about me? Everyone will know we had problems. Part of my label now says I'm a failure." With all the social media today, it's more difficult than ever to maintain the privacy you may want. No one wants to be the topic of discussion on Facebook or Twitter.

Fears such as these can be almost more debilitating than the fear of death. Fear disables. Fear shortens life. Fear cripples relationships. Fear hinders your relationship with God. Fear makes life a daunting chore. Fear keeps you from experiencing God's blessings because it short-circuits your choices and keeps you from growing through change. You still have freedom in Christ, yet you may be walking through life in a mobile prison of fear.

Fear can cause you to imagine the worst possible outcome of your efforts, especially in a divorce. It can limit the development of alternatives and put brakes on pursuing them. To protect yourself from the disappointments that might occur if your efforts don't work out, you settle for less. Your dreams and hopes fade.

Fear also has a warning effect. It cautions you to be wary and hinders what you believe you can do to move ahead in positive ways. Unchecked fear destroys the reality of what might have been.[34]

Fear keeps you from saying, "I can," "I will," "I'm able"—or even "*God* is able." Whenever you give in to your fears, they grow larger, become more real, and finally keep you from being the dreamer and visionary you were created to be.[35] Does any of this fit where you are?

The list of fears just seems to continue . . .

- How do I make good decisions in these areas I never had to make decisions before?
- How do I select an attorney or therapist or apartment and . . . (It helps to make a list and add to it whenever a fear comes to mind.)
- How do I make it financially?

- How do I learn to function as a single parent? I'm afraid of labeling my children, or not having enough time with them.
- Who is safe to talk to?
- I'm afraid of being out of control.
- I'm afraid of my friends rejecting me.
- I'm afraid of going to court.
- I'm afraid my ex will take advantage of me.
- I'm afraid of being alone the rest of my life.
- I'm afraid of where I'll have to live.
- And how do I handle all of my hurt?[36]

The Bible, of course, says a lot about fear—specifically, why God's love and power and His ability to know exactly what needs to be done ought to free us from being crippled and immobilized by fear.

Do not fear, for I am with you; do not be afraid, for I am your God. I will strengthen you; I will help you; I will hold on to you with My righteous right hand. (Isa. 41:10)

I will be with you when you pass through the waters, and when you pass through the rivers, they will not overwhelm you. You will not be

scorched when you walk through the fire, and
the flame will not burn you. (Isa. 43:2)

One kind of fear that's worth specific mention is
worry. It's what we create when we elongate fear with
two things: anticipation and memory. We then infuse
it with our imagination and feed it with emotion.[37]

The word *worry* comes from an Anglo-Saxon root
meaning "to strangle" or "to choke." It is the uneasy,
suffocating feeling you often experience in times of
fear, trouble, or problems. When you worry, you
look pessimistically into the future and think of the
worst possible outcomes. Intense worry is about as
useful to our thinking as a lighted match in a dyna-
mite factory.

Worry is what we get from turning our thinking
into poisoned thoughts. It's been described as a small
trickle of fear that meanders through the mind until
it cuts a channel into which all other thoughts are
drained. That's how it achieves its ability to control.
Worry is always asking the question, "What if . . . ?"
and then answering it in a negative way, such as . . .

- What if I can't learn to be a single person?
- What if I can't make it financially?

The cure for worry is to take every "what if" and turn it around. Replace it with what you *can* do!

- What if I *can* learn to make it as a single person?
- What if I *can* make it financially?

Those are hopeful statements. Try doing this for every fear, and note the difference.

Here's another suggestion. Take a blank index card, and on one side write the word *STOP* in large, bold letters. On the other side, write the complete text of Philippians 4:6–9 (I especially like the *Amplified Bible, Classic Edition* translation because it's so descriptive of how God guards our heart with His peace, and how we guard our own minds by what we choose to think about.) Keep the card with you at all times. Whenever you're alone and begin to worry, take the card out, hold the *STOP* side in front of you, and say that word aloud—"Stop!"— twice with emphasis. Then turn the card over and read the Scripture passage aloud—again, twice with emphasis.

Taking out the card interrupts your thought pattern of fear and worry. Saying "Stop!" further breaks your automatic pattern of worry. Then reading the

Word of God aloud becomes the positive substitute for worry. Even if you must do it silently, depending on your surroundings, you are taking charge of what's seeking to dominate and paralyze you.

You can break the domination of fear and worry. This is God's promise to you.

Chapter 12

Letting Go and Disengaging

At one point or another, you will hear others say, "You need to let go and move on." Their timing in such a suggestion is often off. It's out of sync with what you want or need to hear at the time. At first you may bristle at someone else telling you what to do. After all, they're not where you are.

But what if it really *is* time? What if you've been grieving and waiting long enough? What if instead of someone else saying it, *you're* the one needing to tell yourself to pick up the pieces and get on with your life? Which piece would you pick up first?

That's where it begins—one piece at a time. What can you do today to begin moving on? What will you do tomorrow and the day after?

Many find letting go difficult. Initiators typically let go sooner than Responders, probably because most of them started letting go even before they left. But in order to move forward after you're certain the divorce is unstoppable, it's important to let go of all your emotional feelings in the relationship, both positive and negative—not only your feelings of loving attachment, but also your anger, as well as regrets, unfulfilled expectations, the lifestyle you had, even your old routine. The question to consider is, "Have you let go, or are you still investing emotionally in a relationship that has died?" One author suggests performing sort of a mental autopsy on the dead relationship to discover why it failed and what needs to be changed.[38]

But other things can also form an equally strong measure of attachment for you and can be strangely hard to relinquish. These may include things like gifts from your spouse or from his or her side of the family, as well as other possessions and personal property, such as items you purchased together. Sometimes in a divorce, objects can become a bit of an obsession, a tangible part of the power struggle. Having strong feelings like these is actually fairly normal, but it's worth recognizing and asking questions about these sources of attachment. What are some items still in your possession that keep you thinking about your spouse? Were each of these pieces so important to you prior to knowing that you would be divorcing? Are they benefiting you now in some way? Or they actually just creating more pain, despite your reticence to part with them?

We touched on this subject during an earlier chapter on memories, but it bears repeating. You don't necessarily need to throw things out at this time; you may later wish you'd kept them. But at least put away some of them where, when the situation has cooled and become more settled, you can bring them back out if you want. This may sound strange— grieving over things—but it's actually rather healthy and can be effective in helping you to move on. Even though you may be struggling financially and can hardly replace everything in the house, even the effort of rearranging the furniture and making other minor retouches, especially in the bedroom, can give you a fresher, more renewed perspective.

Most therapists suggest looking at "letting go" across several areas: emotionally, physically, psychologically, and spiritually. Also important is deciding how you will be handling contact with your ex, such as calls, letters, and electronic communication, as well as how you want to handle incidental contact with him or her at the store, at church, and other places where running into each other is unavoidable. Patterns are hard to change, of course, especially after all the time you spent together as a couple. This person filled your life, and you filled theirs. But plan ahead how you intend to handle interactions going forward, and verbally rehearse what you will say and do when it happens.

Even something as formal as a written contract with yourself may be a useful protection to your heart at this time. Declare in writing that you will not engage your ex. Certainly stop talking or texting, sending them e-mails, and searching for them on Facebook or similar points of curiosity. Stop contacting. Stop communicating. In any way.

It's also much easier to maintain these resolutions when you're committed to a group of responsible friends who can assist you in not making contact. You will need accountability. (All of us do!) Don't try doing everything yourself without the support of others.

Even more unavoidable are the moments when your ex will invade the privacy of your mind. What are some ways you'd like to take charge of handling that? How much time do you spend right now, thinking or fantasizing about your former spouse? Is it painful to think of them? Wishful thinking? Are the thoughts sometimes romantic and sexual? Are they more often full of anger and revenge? What is your plan for overcoming or controlling your thinking? Much of your discomfort and longing will come from your thought life, and you should determine now your strategy for coping with it.

Many people want to retain a friendship with their former wife or husband. Most of the time, however, this is an exercise in futility. Why would friendship work when the marriage didn't work? Sometimes we're just too accustomed to companionship. But even if your ex wants a friendship, you are not obligated to agree. It's all right *not* to be friends.

Still others desire a moment of *final closure*. They feel the need to say some things or hear some things. But certain questions can probably never be answered. Often what you'd hear, if your spouse were to try, wouldn't make sense or be sufficient. But it's all right not to have all the answers. Try as you might, you cannot fix your ex, nor can you fix their thinking. All you can control is yourself and your own reactions. The truth is, this type of "final closure" conversation usually only leads to more blame and more arguments. But if you must attempt it . . .

It's important that you stop your side of the arguments as well. Don't ask for justifications for present or past behavior or say how much you've been hurt. Yes, there are things you want this person to think about, but it's not healthy for you to expend energy trying to convince someone who refuses to be convinced. Save yourself the trouble. Everyone will be happier in the end. If you let go of this person and your need to control or condemn, you will be free to find someone whose thinking is compatible with yours.[39]

Some decide to stay in contact because they want to be available for reconciliation or because, they say, "I need to get some things from my ex," or "I need to give some things back"—but again, these are typically nothing more than delays in what either one of you needs right now. Catch yourself when you're tempted to reach out. You may think your reasons for doing so are good, but *are* they? Really?

For years, I've suggested journaling or longhand writing as a way of draining the difficult memories and emotions that can keep you stuck and delaying the healing process. Journaling is a form of draining.

Once you write out what you're thinking or feeling, clarity begins to emerge. Many have also used journaling as a means of identifying their feelings, their motives for making contact, their excuses, and what they will do to counter their desire to reach out. Whenever you want to reach out, always—and I do mean *always*—insert a delay in there, and then identify three things you could do in place of reaching out. Here are some suggestions you can ask yourself:

- How was this desire to contact them triggered?
- What are you feeling? Are you anxious, bored, sad, empty, or lonely?
- Is there a specific thing (thought, memory, or question) driving your desire to connect?
- What outcome do you expect?
- Where are your expectations coming from? Are they fantasies of what you want to have happen? Or are they based upon what has happened in the past? Are you operating from fantasy or reality?
- Are you trying to change the past?
- Are you trying to get a certain reaction?
- Are you trying to relieve the pain and the pressure?

- Do you think negative attention is better than no attention at all?
- Do you feel forgotten? Unimportant? Is contact your way to let the person know you still exist?
- Are you thinking you can control your ex's moving-on process?
- Are you hoping your ex can't really move on as long as you are buzzing around in the background?
- What is your motive?
- Why are you so focused on this one person?[40]

Then finally, here are a few questions that can help you determine your current state of mind and heart. Try pulling out these questions at the beginning of each month throughout the entire first year after divorce to evaluate your growth.

- Have I really let go of my former spouse?
- Do I find myself thinking of my ex-spouse only occasionally?
- Do I feel emotionally upset when I do think of him or her?
- Am I still making excuses to talk to my former spouse?

- Do I still feel bound to a romantic relationship with my spouse?
- Am I overly sensitive to others' opinions?
- What have I learned from the mistakes I made in my marriage?
- What have I done to change?
- Do I see myself growing and becoming a stronger and wiser person?
- How do I feel about my life after divorce?
- Am I truly content with what's left to me after the settlement?[41]

Letting go means taking the energy and emotional investments that were important in your marriage relationship and beginning to invest them elsewhere. Start shifting your focus. Letting go is leaving behind this person you've lost so you're free to move on. And as hard as the reality can be for you to take or accept—probably harder than anything you've ever done in life so far—now is the time. Easy? No. Necessary? Yes.

God bless you and keep you and continually guide you by His Word and His Spirit as you take this courageous step forward into the rest of your life.

Notes

1. See https://www.poets.org/poetsorg/poem/dreams, accessed December 1, 2016.

2. Marilyn Willett Heavelin, *When Your Dreams Die* (San Bernardino, CA: Here's Life, 1990), 30–31.

3. Melvin Belli and Mel Krantlzer, *Divorcing: The Complete Guide for Men and Women* (New York: St. Martin's Paperbacks, 1992), 39.

4. Joseph Warren Kniskern, *When the Vow Breaks* (Nashville: Broadman & Holman, 2008), 7.

5. Ibid., 8.

6. Steve Grissom and Kathy Leonard, *DivorceCare: Hope, Help, and Healing During and After Your Divorce* (Nashville: Thomas Nelson, 2006), 48.

7. Genevieve Clapp, Ph.D., *Divorce and New Beginnings* (New York: John Wiley & Sons, Inc., 2000), 28.

8. Ibid., 17, 37.

9. Ibid., 15.

10. Dr. Bruce Fisher and Dr. Robert Alberti, *Rebuilding When Your Relationship Ends* (Atascadero, CA: Impact Publishing, 2006), 24.

11. David Ziegler, *Traumatic Experience and the Brain* (Gilbert, AZ: Acacia Publishing, 2004), 32.

12. Dr. Zev Wanderer and Tracy Cabot, *Letting Go* (New York: Dell Publishers, 1978), 35.

13. Ibid., 34–38.

14. Susan J. Elliott, *Getting Past Your Breakup* (Jackson, TN: Da Capo Lifelong Press, 2009), 139–140.

15. Wanderer and Cabot, *Letting Go*, 38.

16. Debbie Ford, *Spiritual Divorce* (New York: HarperOne, 2001), 3.

17. Doug Manning, *Don't Take My Grief Away from Me* (San Francisco: Harper, 1979), 41.

18. Ford, *Spiritual Divorce*, 80.

19. Grissom and Leonard, *DivorceCare*, 42.

20. Kniskern, *When the Vow Breaks*, 156–162.

21. Therese Rando, *Grieving: How to Go On Living When Someone You Love Dies* (Lexington, MA: Lexington Books, 1988), 11–12.

22. Ibid., 18–19.

23. Bob Diets, *Life After Loss* (Tuscon, AZ: Fisher Books, 1988), 27.

24. H. Norman Wright, *When the Past Won't Let You Go* (Eugene, OR: Harvest House, 2016), 114–16.

25. Fisher and Alberti, *Rebuilding*, 120–21.

26. Grissom and Leonard, *DivorceCare*, 312.

27. Ibid., 35.

28. Ibid., 37–38.

29. Ibid., 33.

30. Fisher and Alberti, *Rebuilding*, 111.

31. Clapp, *Divorce and New Beginnings*, 54.

32. H. Norman Wright, *Winning Over Your Emotions* (Eugene, OR: Harvest House, 1998), 74.

33. Maggie Scarf, *Unfinished Business: Pressure Points in the Lives of Women* (New York: Doubleday, 1985), 86–87.

34. Sidney Simon, Ph.D., *Getting Unstuck* (New York: Warner Books, 1988), 175–79.

35. Wright, *Winning Over Your Emotions*, 82.

36. Fisher and Alberti, *Rebuilding*, 44–47.

37. Edward M. Hallowell, *Worry* (New York: Pantheon Books, 1997), 67.

38. Fisher and Alberti, *Rebuilding*, 14.

39. Elliott, *Getting Past Your Breakup,* 36.

40. Ibid., 46–47.

41. Kniskern, *When the Vow Breaks*, 325–353.

ADDITIONAL RESOURCES

At one time or another, we will all find ourselves facing a dark journey—the passage through grief. *Experiencing Grief* is written for a person who is in the wake of despair grief leaves.

ISBN: 9780805430929

No matter the details, divorce is not a one cut injury. It is a dark journey that a person travels—but does not have to travel alone. *Experiencing Divorce* is written for the person who is in the wake of despair divorce leaves.

ISBN: 9781433650253

How do you grieve for someone who is still physically with you? *Experiencing Dementia* is written for the person who is in the wake of despair that the diagnosis of Dementia brings.

ISBN: 9781433650239